TopReaders

American Indians

Robert Coupe

Contents

American Indians lived right across North America long before people from England and Europe arrived.

First Americans

The first Americans came from Asia. About 15,000 years ago, they followed herds of animals across land and arrived in Alaska.

Later the sea rose.
It covered the land they
had crossed. They continued
to follow the animals right
through North America.

Across the Water

People fished and carried goods in boats and canoes. They made them out of logs, animal skins, or reeds.

bullboat

This painted canoe was used in ceremonies. The bear is an Indian dressed in a costume.

Across the Land

People who lived on the Plains moved around on horses. They followed the buffalo that they hunted.

As they traveled, mothers carried their babies in papooses.

eagle
feathers

Plains pony

Hunting Wild Ducks

Indians used reeds and feathers to make imitation ducks. They put these in ponds. Real ducks flew in to join them.

Indians made nets
to trap wild ducks.
They also caught
some ducks with
their bare hands.

Hunting Buffalo

On horseback, Indians chased herds of buffalo. They killed them with spears and arrows.

Indians ate buffalo meat. They used hides for clothing. They burnt buffalo fat in lamps.

Clothes

In cold places, Indians wore clothes made from things around them. Most clothes fitted very loosely.

Pants, parkas , and boots were made from the skins of caribou and seals.

Plains women made moccasins and other clothes from leather and plant material.

moccasins

Sport

Indian men needed to be strong and fast so that they could be good hunters and fighters. Sports helped to keep them fit and strong.

Stickball was a fast and violent game. Groups of men who were quarreling often played against each other.

Special Occasions

For some ceremonies, people wore decorated robes. Kwakiutl dancers wore costumes made of cedar bark and bird masks made of wood.

Kwakiutl dancers

Headdresses
were made
from eagles'
feathers.

Rain and Snow Dances

Hopi Indians held snake ceremonies in order to bring rain. Afterward, they took the snakes back to the desert.

Objibwa hunter

An Objibwa hunter dances to celebrate a snowfall. Now his prey will be easier to catch.

Cooking a Meal

Every day, Indian women spent hours collecting food and water. Their daughters helped them prepare meals for the tribe.

These Cheyenne women are cooking a stew. Hot stones heat up the food in the pot.

Tepees

Indians on the Plains lived in tents called tepees. They were made of the skins of buffalo. People folded and carried the tepees when they moved.

People cooked food over a fireplace inside their tepee. The smoke went out through smoke flaps at the top.

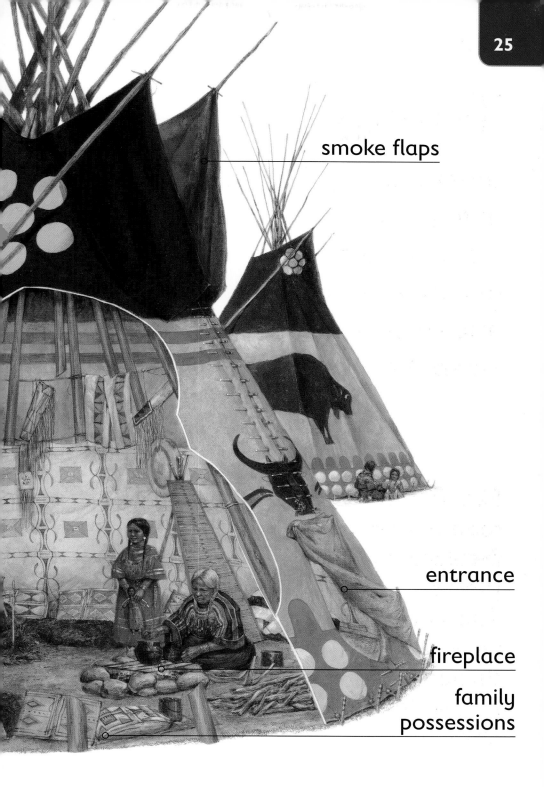

smoke flaps

entrance

fireplace

family
possessions

Village Life

People in the Southwest lived in villages called pueblos. Houses were stacked up one on top of the other. They were strongly built of stone and mud-brick.

The people who lived above ground level reached their houses by climbing up long wooden ladders.

Indians Today

After Europeans came, Indians lost their lands. Some tribes died out. Now, the number of Indians is growing. Some tribes are getting back their lands.

Clay pots are examples of Indian craft.

Dancers, singers, and craftspeople come to meetings called powwows in many places across North America.

Quiz

Can you match the pictures with their names?

tepees   pony

clay pot   bullboat

Glossary

caribou: large deer. In some countries caribou are called reindeer.

Cheyenne: belonging to a tribe that lived on the Plains

Hopi: belonging to a tribe from the Southwest

Kwakiutl: belonging to a tribe that lived on the west coast of North America

moccasins: soft leather shoes with no heel

Objibwa: belonging to a tribe that lived in the northern part of North America

papooses: kinds of bags used for carrying babies on people's backs

parkas: jackets with long sleeves and hoods

Plains: flat regions in North America

powwows: gatherings of American Indians

Southwest: a region, north of Mexico, where several Indian tribes lived

Index